New York

BY ANN HEINRICHS

Content Adviser: Jendy Murphy, Head of the Children's Department, Albany Public Library Main Branch, Albany, New York

Reading Adviser: Dr. Linda D. Labbo, Department of Reading Education, College of Education, The University of Georgia

COMPASS POINT BOOKS   MINNEAPOLIS, MINNESOTA

Compass Point Books
3109 West 50th Street, #115
Minneapolis, MN 55410

Visit Compass Point Books on the Internet at *www.compasspointbooks.com*
or e-mail your request to *custserv@compasspointbooks.com*

Editors: E. Russell Primm, Emily J. Dolbear, and Catherine Neitge
Photo Researcher: Svetlana Zhurkina
Photo Selector: Linda S. Koutris
Designer: The Design Lab
Cartographer: XNR Productions, Inc.

Library of Congress Cataloging-in-Publication Data
Heinrichs, Ann.
    New York / by Ann Heinrichs.
        v. cm.— (This land is your land)
    Includes bibliographical references (p.   ) and index.
    Contents: Welcome to New York!—Mountains, rivers, and lakes—A trip through time—Government
by the people—New Yorkers at work—Getting to know New Yorkers—Let's explore New York!
    ISBN 0-7565-0311-6
    1. New York (State)—Juvenile literature. [1. New York (State)] I. Title.
    F119.3 .H45 2002
    974.7—dc21   2002002962

Table of Contents

▲ Even though New York is known for busy cities, most of the state is rural and beautifully scenic.

"I love New York!" This slogan shows up everywhere in New York. You see it on T-shirts, bumper stickers, and mugs. A big, red heart stands in the place of the word love.

And New Yorkers do love their state. Some love it because of New York City. It's the largest, busiest city in the country. Others love New York State for its small, quiet villages. They enjoy its deep forests and sparkling lakes. New Yorkers are proud of their history, too. New York City was the first capital of the United States.

For baseball fans, New York is tops. It's the home of the New York Yankees and the New York Mets. For those who love nature, New York is a wonderland of natural beauty.

See what you think as you explore New York. You'll discover your own special reasons to say, "I love New York!"

Mountains, Rivers, and Lakes

▲ Taughannock Falls is located in New York's Finger Lakes region.

To many people, "New York" means New York City. But New York State is much more than a big city. It's a land of mountains, rivers, lakes, and rolling farmland.

New York is located in the northeastern United States. In size, it ranks thirtieth among the states. Canada and Lake Ontario lie to the north. To the south are New Jersey and Pennsylvania. Vermont, Massachusetts, and Connecticut run along New York's eastern edge. New York's southeast corner faces the Atlantic Ocean. Lake Erie and Canada are on the west.

The Appalachian Mountains cover the western half of New York. Within this region are the Catskill Mountains and the Finger Lakes. These eleven lakes are long and thin, like fingers. Many rivers run through this area. Dairy cows graze across the grassy river valleys.

The Hudson River runs down eastern New York. It flows into the Atlantic Ocean at New York City. Manhattan Island is New York City's main business center. Staten Island and Long Island are very near Manhattan.

Albany, the state capital, lies along the Hudson River. Near Albany, the Mohawk River branches off the Hudson to the west. Early settlers followed these two rivers as they explored new parts of the state.

▲ The Adirondack Mountains in autumn

Lakes Ontario and Erie are two of America's Great Lakes. Between them are the spectacular Niagara Falls. Farmers along the Great Lakes grow apple and cherry trees.

Lake Ontario flows into the St. Lawrence River. The St. Lawrence pours into the Atlantic Ocean.

The Adirondack Mountains are in northern New York. People love to go camping, hiking, and skiing there. New York's highest point, Mount Marcy, is in the Adirondacks. Long, thin Lake Champlain forms the border between New York and Vermont.

Forests cover more than half of New York State. Deer, beavers, and bears live in the forests. Cottontail

▲ This black bear is one of many animals that live in New York's forests.

rabbits and snowshoe hares scamper through them, too. Bluebirds are the state bird. They became scarce in the

1950s. By now, however, they have made a comeback.

Southern New York has warm summers and cool winters. Farther north, winters can be very cold. Even in summer, the Adirondacks stay cool. Heavy snow falls on Buffalo every winter. The Adirondacks are snowy, too. But that's good news if you like skiing and bobsledding.

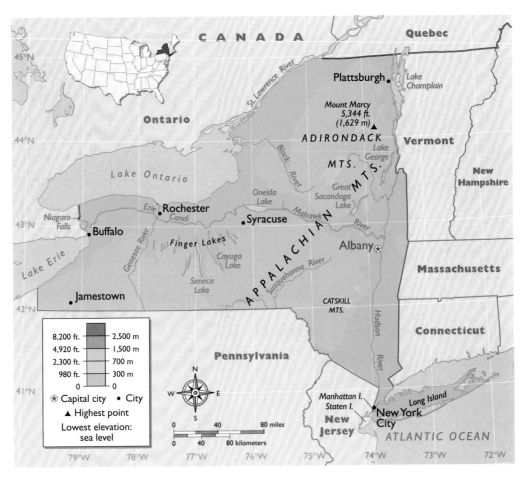

▲ A topographic map of New York

In the past, many Native Americans lived in New York. The Iroquois lived in the northern woodlands. They were a brotherhood of five tribes. Iroquois homes were **longhouses.** Many families lived in each one. Villages often held councils, or meetings, to make group decisions.

▲ Indians lived in villages like this one on Manhattan Island before European settlers arrived.

▲ The Hudson River is named after Henry Hudson.

Several Algonquian groups also lived in New York. The Mahican lived in the Hudson River Valley. *Mahican* is an Indian word meaning "wolf." The Montauk farmed and fished on Long Island.

Giovanni da Verrazzano may have been the first European to visit the New York area. He was an Italian working for France. Verrazzano may have sailed into the Hudson River in 1524. Next, Henry Hudson came from the Netherlands. In 1609, he sailed up the river that is now named after him.

Soon colonists from the Netherlands, called the Dutch, arrived. They named their **colony** New Netherland. In 1624, they founded Fort Orange. It was the first European settlement

▲ Fort Orange was the first European settlement in New York.

in New York. Today, this site is known as Albany. Other Dutch
settlers set up New Amsterdam in 1625. The British took over
New Netherland in 1664. They changed the colony's name to
New York. New Amsterdam became today's New York City.

▲ American colonists won the Battle of Saratoga.

New Yorkers joined the other American colonists in the Revolutionary War (1775–1783). The Battle of Saratoga took place in New York. After the colonists' victory, France decided to help them fight the British. In 1788, New York became the eleventh U.S. state. New York City was the new nation's capital from 1785 until 1790.

Many new settlers poured into the area to farm the rich soil. Busy factories grew up in cities along the rivers and lakes. Soon New York was the country's center for manufacturing and trade.

In the 1880s, thousands of **immigrants** began arriving in New York. They passed the Statue of Liberty. It was the symbol of freedom to all. New York City became a "melting pot" for people from dozens of nations.

▲ Immigrants from countries around the world have passed through Ellis Island, and hundreds of thousands eventually settled in New York City.

After World War II (1939–1945), New York City was chosen as the home of the United Nations. People of all nations began meeting there to discuss world problems. Meanwhile, New York continued to grow. The state government worked hard to give its people good roads, schools, and jobs.

Disaster struck New York City in 2001. **Terrorists** crashed airplanes into the twin towers of the World Trade Center. Thousands of people were killed in the attack. New Yorkers pulled together and helped one another to carry on. They proved that they were strong and full of hope for the future.

▲ **Emergency workers at the World Trade Center disaster site**

Government by the People

Even children can take part in government. Students in North Syracuse proved that. They wanted the apple muffin to be their state muffin. They wrote letters to the governor—and it worked! The apple muffin **bill** was passed in 1987.

▲ The New York state capitol

New York's state government has three branches—
executive, legislative, and judicial. The executive branch
carries out the state's laws. New York's governor heads the
executive branch. Voters elect the governor to a four-year
term. The secretary of state, lieutenant governor, and
attorney general help with other executive jobs.

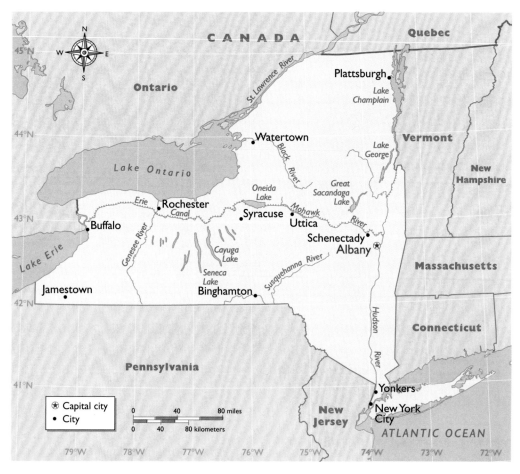

▲ **A geopolitical map of New York**

The legislative branch makes the state laws. New York's lawmakers serve in the state legislature in Albany. It has two parts, called houses—a 61-member senate and a 150-member assembly. Members serve a two-year term. They vote on about 2,000 items every year!

The judicial branch is the court system. It is made up of judges. They decide whether someone has broken the law. New York's supreme court has more than 300 judges.

▲ **A rural New York county courthouse**

However, the state's highest court is the court of appeals.

New York is divided into sixty-two counties. Five of

▲ Former first lady Hillary Rodham Clinton is
one of the two senators from New York.

these counties are the five **boroughs** of New York City—Manhattan (New York County), Brooklyn (Kings County), Queens (Queens County), the Bronx (Bronx County), and Staten Island (Richmond County). County officials are in charge of highways, libraries, and parks. Most cities elect a mayor and a city council.

New Yorkers are proud of their leaders. Four U.S. presidents were born in New York. They were Martin Van Buren, Millard Fillmore, Theodore Roosevelt, and Franklin D. Roosevelt. Former first lady Hillary Rodham Clinton became a U.S. senator from New York in 2000.

New Yorkers at Work

Take a peek at your favorite magazine. You'll find the publisher's name and address in the first few pages. Chances are, the publisher is based in New York. New York makes more books, magazines, and newspapers than any other state.

▲ New York is a world fashion center. The clothing industry is centered in the garment district.

▲ A truck full of red, ripe New York apples

Chemicals are another important product. They include medicines, soap, and paint. Factories in Rochester make cameras, film, copy machines, and electronics. New Yorkers also make food products, car and airplane parts, and clothing. New York City is the nation's center for women's fashions.

New York's farmers are busy, too. Milk is the state's major farm product, and apples are its leading fruit. Settlers brought apple seeds to New York in the 1600s. They dried apples so they could eat them during the winter. New York ranks second in the nation in its production of apples and maple syrup. It's third in milk and grapes and fourth in meat.

So far, we've noted New York's products. But four of every five New York workers have service jobs. Many of them work in restaurants or stores. Some are health care workers, teachers, or actors. Others work in banks and other **financial** businesses. New York City is a world center for money-related trades.

▲ **The New York Stock Exchange is one option for people interested in money-related jobs.**

▲ Dr. Jonas Salk created the first polio vaccine.

New York's scientists and inventors have made life better for us all. George Eastman invented film that comes in rolls instead of hard plates. Linus Yale invented the locks we have on our doors. Jonas Salk created a **vaccine** that prevents polio, a crippling disease. Today, that vaccine is helping children around the world.

"New York is a meeting place for every race in the world."
Federico Garcia Lorca, a visiting writer, said this in 1932,
and it's still true today.

Immigrants from many lands settled in New York. They
came from Italy, Ireland, Britain, Russia, and other nations.
Almost 3 million residents have roots in Spanish-speaking

▲ New York City is home to people from nearly every country of the world.

countries. Their homelands include Puerto Rico, Mexico, Cuba, and Haiti. No other state has more African-American citizens. About 3 million African-Americans live in New York. Another 1 million New Yorkers are Asian. They came from China, India, Korea, the Philippines, and Japan.

▲ African-Americans gather in Harlem to support South African leader Nelson Mandela.

▲ Buffalo is one of New York's largest cities—as well as one of its snowiest!

In 2000, almost 19 million people lived in New York. Only California and Texas have more people. Four of every five New Yorkers live in or near cities. The largest cities are New York City, Buffalo, and Rochester. More people live in New York City than in any other city in the United States.

▲ The Macy's Thanksgiving Day Parade is enjoyed by television viewers around the world.

New York City has great parades. The Macy's Thanksgiving Day Parade and the Saint Patrick's Day Parade are
favorites. The city is also a world-class music and theater

center. It's no wonder that so many New Yorkers are in show business. Humphrey Bogart and Tom Cruise became movie stars. The Marx Brothers, Woody Allen, and Rosie O'Donnell made people laugh. George Gershwin and Billy Joel wrote music, and Lena Horne sang.

▲ The Marx Brothers were famous New York entertainers.

Many beloved writers also lived in New York. Washington Irving wrote tales based on folk legends. One of his stories tells about Rip Van Winkle who took a nap for twenty years. James Fenimore Cooper told about New York's **frontier** days. Herman Melville wrote *Moby Dick,* about a giant whale. Many African-American writers became famous during the Harlem Renaissance. That movement began in New York City's Harlem community in the 1920s.

▲ **New York's Harlem community in 1925**

▲ New York Mets fans come together to support their favorite team.

New Yorkers are wild about baseball. Entire families and neighborhoods take sides. They're either New York Yankees fans or New York Mets fans. By 2001, the Yankees had won the World Series twenty-six times!

▲ Hundreds of thousands of immigrants passed through Ellis Island before it closed. Today it has been restored and is a museum.

No one can see all of New York in just one visit. But New York City is a good place to start. You can see for miles from the top of the Empire State Building. You can climb the stairs to the top of the Statue of Liberty. New immigrants once landed in nearby Ellis Island.

It's easy to explore New York's "melting pot" of **cultures.** Just stroll through Little Italy and Chinatown. In Brooklyn, you can visit Italian, Russian, and Middle Eastern neighborhoods.

▲ Restaurants are a popular destination in New York City's Chinatown.

Have you ever wondered where your food goes after you eat it? You'll find out at the Children's Museum of Manhattan. You can climb through a huge mouth and follow the food's path. You can even "go down the wrong pipe" and visit the lungs!

▲ There are many ways to have fun at the Children's Museum of Manhattan.

▲ **Theodore Roosevelt helped design Sagamore Hill, his home for most of his life.**

Out on Long Island, visit Sagamore Hill. It was President Theodore Roosevelt's home. His many odd belongings are still there. Alongside Long Island is Fire Island. This seaside wilderness is protected as a national seashore.

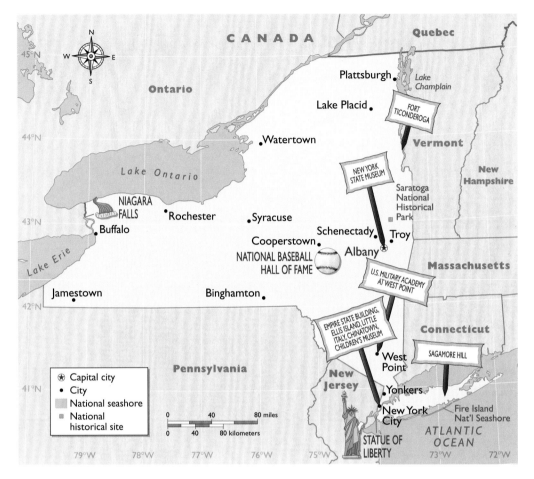

▲ **Places to visit in New York**

At the state capitol in Albany, you can watch lawmakers at work. When they vote, you'll know the score right away. Their votes appear on a huge electronic "scoreboard." Don't miss Albany's New York State Museum. There you'll see a life-sized Iroquois longhouse. Another exhibit shows New York's wilderness in prehistoric times.

What is it like to be in the army? Do you want the modern answer or the historic one? At the U.S. Military Academy in West Point, you can watch today's **cadets** training. Then

▲ The U.S. Military Academy is located at West Point.

▲ Fort Ticonderoga

you can travel back in time at Fort Ticonderoga or Saratoga National Historical Park. Both sites show how soldiers lived in the 1700s.

If you like hiking and camping, you'll love the Adirondacks. New York has declared much of this region "forever wild." Its deep woods and rugged mountains are truly wilderness country. Lake Placid is a center for winter sports. Many skiing and ice-skating stars train there.

How much do you know about baseball? You can test yourself at the National Baseball Hall of Fame in Cooperstown. Visitors are invited to take part in baseball **trivia** games.

▲ **Felix Gottwald of Austria performs a jump at the 2000 Winter Goodwill Games in Lake Placid.**

They also see uniforms, bats, and films of baseball's greatest stars. West of Cooperstown is the Finger Lakes region. It's a wonderland of lakes, forests, and historic villages.

Every year, 10 million people visit Niagara Falls. Why not join them? From the top of the falls, you can watch the water plunge over the cliffs. Or you can take a boat ride along the roaring waters at the bottom. Either way, you'll say, "I love New York!"

▲ Niagara Falls straddles the border between New York and Canada.

Important Dates

1609 Henry Hudson sails into what is now called the Hudson River.

1624 Dutch settlers establish Fort Orange (Albany), the first permanent European settlement in New York.

1788 New York becomes the eleventh U.S. state.

1825 The Erie Canal opens, allowing ships to sail from the Hudson River to the Great Lakes.

1883 The Brooklyn Bridge is completed—the world's longest bridge at that time.

1886 The Statue of Liberty is dedicated in New York harbor.

1901 President William McKinley is assassinated in Buffalo, and Theodore Roosevelt is sworn in as president.

1939– 1940 New York holds a World's Fair at Flushing Meadows.

1959 The St. Lawrence Seaway opens to ocean-going ships.

1980 The Winter Olympic Games are held in Lake Placid.

2001 Terrorists destroy the 110-story twin towers of New York City's World Trade Center.

Glossary

bill—a proposed law

boroughs—sections of a city

cadets—students in a military school

colony—a territory that belongs to the country that settles it

cultures—groups of people who share beliefs, customs, and a way of life

financial—related to money

frontier—an area that is not yet explored or settled

immigrants—people who come to another country to live

longhouses—long buildings where many Iroquois families lived

terrorists—people who use violence and fear to further their cause

trivia—small details or little-known facts

vaccine—a medicine that prevents a disease

Did You Know?

★ Adirondack State Park is larger than Yellowstone, Yosemite, Grand Canyon, Glacier, and Olympic National Parks combined.

★ About 600,000 gallons (2.3 million liters) of water flow over Niagara Falls every second. That's enough water to fill about 9,000 bathtubs a second. One second of water would fill your bathtub once a day for almost twenty-five years!

★ It took thirty-one years (1867–1898) to build the state capitol in Albany.

★ New York is sometimes called the Big Apple. The name comes from jazz musicians in the 1930s. They used the term "apple" for any city. To play in New York City was really the big time. So they called it the Big Apple.

★ The Empire State Building opened in 1931. It was the world's tallest building for forty years.

★ New York had more people than any other U.S. state from 1810 to 1962.

★ The area north of New York City is called Upstate New York.

State capital: Albany

State motto: *Excelsior* (Latin for "Ever Upward")

State nickname: The Empire State

Statehood: July 26, 1788; eleventh state

Area: 49,112 square miles (127,200 sq km); **rank:** thirtieth

Highest point: Mount Marcy, 5,344 feet (1,629 m)

Lowest point: Sea level, along the Atlantic coast

Highest recorded temperature: 108°F (42°C) at Troy on July 22, 1926

Lowest recorded temperature: −52°F (−47°C) at Old Forge on February 18, 1979

Average January temperature: 21°F (−6°C)

Average July temperature: 69°F (21°C)

Population in 2000: 18,976,457; **rank:** third

Largest cities in 2000: New York City (8,008,278), Buffalo (292,648), Rochester (219,773), Yonkers (196,086)

Factory products: Chemicals, machinery, computer and electronic equipment, printed material, food products

Farm products: Milk, apples, grapes, vegetables

Mining products: Stone, salt, sand, gravel

State flag: New York's state flag has the state coat of arms on a blue background. The coat of arms shows two ships on a river with a grassy shore. Behind them stands a mountain with the sun rising behind it. Above this scene is an eagle standing on a globe of the world. Two figures stand on each side. They represent Liberty and Justice. Liberty holds the cap of a freed Roman slave. Justice is blindfolded. This shows that justice depends on facts, not on how someone looks. She holds a sword and scales, which stand for fairness. Beneath them is a banner with the state motto, *Excelsior* ("Ever Upward").

State seal: The state seal also shows the state coat of arms.

State abbreviations: N.Y. (traditional): NY (postal)

State Symbols

State bird: Bluebird

State flower: Rose

State tree: Sugar maple

State animal: Beaver

State insect: Ladybug

State fish: Brook trout

State fruit: Apple

State beverage: Milk

State gem: Garnet

State fossil: *Eurypterus remipes*, a relative of the sea scorpion

State shell: Bay scallop

State muffin: Apple muffin

State commemorative quarter: released January 2, 2001

Making New York Apple Muffins

This is a version of the apple muffin recipe developed by school children in North Syracuse.

Makes twenty-four muffins.

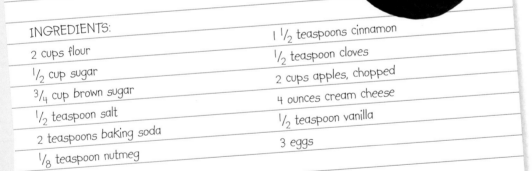

INGREDIENTS:

2 cups flour

1/2 cup sugar

3/4 cup brown sugar

1/2 teaspoon salt

2 teaspoons baking soda

1/8 teaspoon nutmeg

1 1/2 teaspoons cinnamon

1/2 teaspoon cloves

2 cups apples, chopped

4 ounces cream cheese

1/2 teaspoon vanilla

3 eggs

DIRECTIONS:

Preheat oven to 375°. Place muffin papers into the cups of a muffin tin. Combine flour, sugars, salt, baking soda, and spices. Set them aside. Combine apples and the rest of the ingredients in a large bowl. Add the dry ingredients to the apple mixture, a little at a time. Stir until everything is evenly mixed. Do not stir too much! Spoon the muffin mixture into the muffin papers, filling about half full. Bake for 20 to 30 minutes.

"I Love New York"

Words and music by Steve Karmen

I love New York,
I love New York,
I love New York.
There isn't another like it
No matter where you go
And nobody can compare it.
It's win and place and show.
New York is special.
New York is diff'rent
'Cause there's no place else on earth
Quite like New York
And that's why
I love New York,
I love New York,
I love New York.

Woody Allen (1935–) is a movie actor and director. He is famous for his goofy sense of humor. Allen was born in New York City.

Saint Frances Xavier Cabrini (1850–1917) was the first U.S. citizen to be named a saint in the Roman Catholic Church. She founded schools, orphanages, and hospitals. One was New York City's Columbus Hospital. Cabrini was an immigrant from Italy.

Millard Fillmore (1800–1874) was the thirteenth president of the United States from 1850 to 1853. Fillmore was born in Cayuga County, New York.

George Gershwin (1898–1937) wrote music with a truly American flavor. It combined jazz and classical sounds. He was born in Brooklyn.

Washington Irving (1783–1859) wrote stories about New Yorkers and old legends. He was born in New York City.

Mickey Mantle (1931–1995) played baseball for the New York Yankees. He hit 536 home runs and broke many baseball records. Mantle was born in Oklahoma.

Frederic Remington (1861–1909) made paintings and sculptures of cowboys and horses. He was born in Canton.

John Davison Rockefeller (1839–1937) started the Standard Oil Company. He gave millions of dollars to charity and the arts. He was born in Richford.

Franklin Delano Roosevelt (1882–1945) was the thirty-second president of the United States (1933–1945). He was born in Hyde Park.

Theodore Roosevelt (1858–1919) was the twenty-sixth president of the United States (1901–1909). He was born in New York City.

Sojourner Truth (1797–1883) was a powerful speaker against slavery and for women's rights. Her real name was Isabella Baumfree. She was born a slave near Kingston.

Martin Van Buren (1782–1862) was the eighth president of the United States (1837–1841). Van Buren was born in Kinderhook.

At the Library

Bierman, Carol. *Journey to Ellis Island*. New York: Hyperion Press, 1998.

Chambers, Veronica, and B. Marvis. *The Harlem Renaissance*. Broomall, Penn.: Chelsea House, 1997.

Gelman, Amy. *New York*. Minneapolis, Minn.: Lerner Publications, 1992

Quackenbush, Robert M. *Daughter of Liberty: A True Story of the American Revolution*. New York: Hyperion Press, 1999.

Schomp, Virginia. *New York*. Tarrytown, N.Y.: Benchmark Books, 1997.

On the Web

For more information on this topic, use FactHound.

1. Go to *www.facthound.com*
2. Type in this book ID: 0756503116
3. Click on the *Fetch It* button.

FactHound will find the best Web sites for you.

Through the Mail

New York State Department of State
Division of Administrative Rules
41 State Street
Albany, NY 12231
To request free materials about New York

New York State Division of Tourism
One Commerce Plaza
Albany, NY 12245
For information on travel and interesting sights in New York

New York State Museum
Office of Cultural Education
Madison Avenue
Albany, NY 12230
For information on New York's history

On the Road

New York State Capitol
Albany, New York 12224
518/474-2418
To visit New York's state capitol

**New York State Museum
Cultural Education Center**
Empire State Plaza
Madison Avenue
Albany, New York 12230
518/474-5877
To learn more about New York's history and culture

Index

About the Author

Ann Heinrichs grew up in Fort Smith, Arkansas, and lives in Chicago. She is the author of more than sixty books for children and young adults on Asian, African, and U.S. history and culture. Ann has also written numerous newspaper, magazine, and encyclopedia articles. She is an award-winning martial artist, specializing in t'ai chi empty-hand and sword forms.

Ann has traveled widely throughout the United States, Africa, Asia, and the Middle East. In exploring each state for this series, she rediscovered the people, history, and resources that make this a great land, as well as the concerns we share with people around the world.